Confessions of a Pastor's Wife

April Gee
Confessions of a Pastor's Wife

Published by Spines
ISBN 979-8-89691-150-0

Confessions of a Pastor's Wife

MARRIED TO A NARCISSIST

APRIL GEE

Dedication

I dedicate this book to all those who are in or have been in a narcissistic relationship. To those who have choked on tears and pain because the narcissist you're with didn't allow you to cry. To all those who have lost themselves in a relationship and denied themselves love, freedom and peace.

This book is for you. You have a voice. My hope and prayer is that you find You again and begin to live. You are worth living for.

Contents

As I sit here and write this, I am overwhelmed with emotion. I don't know where to really begin because I've held it in for so long. I have suppressed the memories of all the bad things that have happened to me in my marriage, thinking it was the right thing to do. The only result of that is that I wounded myself emotionally and mentally. After much thought, I realized that I needed to tell my story. Not only will it help me, but it can help someone else. I was married to a narcissistic preacher. Being married to a narcissist is not an easy thing. They tear you down, and mess you up mentally and emotionally, and leave you feeling as if you're crazy and a terrible person.

As you read this, I want to encourage you. You can overcome a narcissistic relationship by getting help.

You can be healthy in all areas of your life. Remember, it's not your fault, and you should never blame yourself for someone else's behavior. Keep your head up, keep your faith and keep loving!!

Preface

Confessions of a Pastor's Wife is a short biography of a woman who suffered at the hands of a narcissistic pastor. This woman faces emotional abuse from someone who is supposed to follow God's commands of love and peace. This biography is part one, for there is much more to the story. This book only scratches the surface of the lies, sexual promiscuity, and evilness associated with someone who claims to be the voice of God.

CHAPTER 1

Let's begin

Even from the beginning, my ex-husband was controlling. I didn't recognize the signs because I grew up with a controlling, narcissistic mother. I thought it was the normal way to live. My mother was a controlling woman, always wanting everything her way, wanting things done when she wanted it, with not much room for compromise. To deal with my mother's ways, my two brothers never stayed home much, opting to hang out with their friends. My father wouldn't engage much, he would instead head outside (as most older men used to do). My father would spend most of the day outside building things and not listening to my mom and her rants. Me on the other hand, was always around her because I thought she needed me. I also thought it meant we had a special bond. I was wrong.

The trouble, (as I now understand it) with being under the control of a narcissist is that you don't know they're one at first. You don't recognize the signs, and can't tell what they're doing. Before long, they have you in their grip and it's hell getting loose. You start to believe what they do is normal, and that all people are like this. It's only after someone or some event awakens you that you realize who you're dating, married to, or friends with. For me, I stumbled onto it, after I separated from him. I called it controlling, because I didn't know what a narcissist was.

CHAPTER 2

Narcissist defined

A narcissist is a person who has an excessive interest in or admiration of themselves. He or she wants praise, wants all attention on them, has a sense of self-importance, is arrogant, and lacks empathy. They are envious of others and have a sense of entitlement. A narcissist love bombs a person at first, to pull them in. **Love bombing** is when a person gives you compliments, praises you, adores you and gives you lots and lots of presents, all with the purpose of getting you to trust them. Once you do, they turn on you like a rabid dog (this is their manipulation).

MEETING MY EX-HUSBAND:

I met my ex-husband at Morris College in 2003. He was a preacher, and looking to pastor his first church. I wasn't really looking for a relationship because I had just gotten out of one. My ex approached me after a class we had one day, and asked me out. I didn't say yes at first, and in hindsight, I wish I hadn't said yes at all. After a few times of asking, I did say yes, and we started dating. After about two months of dating, he started complaining about my friends and how much time I was spending with them (Sign 1: separating you from outside influences). He even started complaining about how much time I spent studying (Sign 2: wanting more attention to themselves, I mean it's college, we're supposed to study). Matter of fact he started complaining about almost everything I did. I didn't think much of it at first, I just figured he wanted more time with me. I tried to do this, without neglecting my studies, but it wasn't enough. Eventually, he wore me down with his demands for more attention, and I started neglecting my studies and my friends. I thought I was in love and doing the right thing, but I was so wrong.

I should have known that something was wrong, but I was blind. My grades slipped some, but not much, because I would be adamant at times about studying and I would lie and say I was sick. That's the thing, I started doing things I normally wouldn't do, because I wanted to please him (Sign 3: you're not thinking of your needs but primarily theirs).

Now, let me add this in. Being raised by a narcissistic mother messed up my self-esteem. I was more passive, and felt as if I couldn't speak up for myself. I was also bullied in school, so all of this screwed up my self-esteem. This is not an excuse, but it does explain why I was open to someone else's control. I was basically vulnerable. If you have had these things happen to you, it could explain why you gravitate towards those who are narcissistic. This is an explanation for me, and maybe an explanation for some of you reading this**

CHAPTER 3

Well, back to the program

I did things to please him because he needed that praise, and I fell into it. He ate it up, he loved it, but never returned it back. The love bombs he used to give, he didn't give anymore. Instead, he gave criticisms and not always constructive ones. I was slowly being shaped into what he wanted, a tool that he could use and control for his benefit. These things were the molding stage, his words and his insecurity were instruments.

After college, we got married and ended up moving into his mother's home. Now here's the thing about the wedding, we didn't have one. We got married in his grandfather's living room. My parents didn't know, and neither did his family. I was so stupid to not question this! I needed to have my butt whipped, for real. The real reason he didn't want a wedding (as I found out later) was because he had been such an asshole in his hometown and had lived a terrible life. He didn't want anyone to talk about him or tell me the truth about him.

We couldn't afford our own home for a while, so we ended up living with his mother for a couple of years, which was not fun. My ex had a strained relationship with his mother because she neglected him when he was a child, and often called him terrible names (as he told me). They would get into arguments a lot. My opinion was that it was not only because of what she did when he was young, but also because they were so much alike. They rarely agreed on anything, and whenever she tried to give him advice, he'd get angry and cuss her out. He would often want me to agree with him during the arguments, and would try to push me to argue with his mother like him, but I would choose to stay out of it. He would get angry at this too (by now, you can see that my ex has an anger problem). There was never any winning with him, because again, he's a narcissist; they never see that they're wrong.

During this time, my ex was working as a police officer in the Florence, SC area. He was also searching for a church to pastor. He eventually was hired at a church in the Hartsville, SC area and quit his job to become a full-time pastor. He was very happy to be pastoring, and for just a short time, everything was okay. I had my first daughter while we were still living with his mother, and I was extremely happy. I had always wanted to be a mother, I love children. My daughter gave me sunshine in an otherwise dark world, she is my bright spot and gives me so much joy. I love that wonderful daughter of mine (insert big smile).

Eventually, we were able to move into a home of our own. This came as a result of my ex finding papers at the church that showed how one of the members was stealing money to fix his house. This church member would buy wood to fix different things around the church, but would also use the church's money to buy wood for his house. The paperwork had been left inside the desk in the pastor's office, and when my ex took over as pastor, he discovered it there. He brought it to the church's attention, and in fear of being persecuted, the member offered to give an old house to my ex. It was a fixer-up house, but my ex was skilled in carpentry, so he fixed it himself. I helped as much as I could, because we didn't have money to hire others to help. His mother helped to buy furniture, and appliances for the house, which was a great blessing. Eventually, the house was finished, and we moved in.

Moving into our home should have been a happy time, but it wasn't. Around this time, my dad had gotten sick. He'd been diagnosed with stage 4 prostate cancer, and was getting sicker. The doctor didn't give him long to live, so I was running to my parents' house in Lancaster, SC and back to Hartsville, SC just trying to be there for my parents, and spend as much time as I could with my dad.

My ex was also being voted out of his church at this time too. My ex had a tendency to talk trash to others, as if others were stupid, and he was the only one with sense. He would not listen to others about being more compassionate. Instead, he decided to do what he wanted. He would insult people from the pulpit, calling them names (for example, he called one member predator because she had dreads). The members were tired of him, and wanted him out. They voted him out on the basis of conduct unbecoming of a pastor. I won't say that he deserved all of it, because there were certain members who were stealing money from the church, and didn't want to get prosecuted, but I do believe he deserved some of it.

CHAPTER 4

My Father's Death

Right before my ex was voted out, my father died. I was torn apart, hurting and full of grief. Instead of being supportive, my ex was angry because he knew he was about to be voted out. I understand there was a lot going on at this time, and I was trying to be supportive of my ex and my mother. My attention was split, because I was also tending to my little girl, who at this time was only 3 years old. I needed support too, so I was looking for us to support each other, but this didn't happen. My mother needed my help, my brothers were trying to help as much as possible, but she was leaning on me to keep order and to write the obituary and do all the planning. I was looking at her to do these things and she didn't want to. So, I put the funeral together and continued to support my ex and my mother.

Now, you may think that my mother was overcome with grief, but not in my opinion. In my opinion, she was faking it. The day my dad died, my mother started throwing his things away. The coroner had just taken his body out, and she started going through his stuff and throwing it in the trash. I walked into the room and asked what she was doing, she responded by saying there was no need to keep it because he was dead.

Earlier, she was crying and hollering like a maniac, now she was throwing things away like it was filled with diseases. I told her to stop and wait, dad had just passed, and I wanted to take time to grieve and look through some of his things, keep some for sentimental reasons. This is why I believed her grief was fake. I mention this because I want to point out that I was hurting, and instead of properly grieving, I had to focus on what my ex-husband wanted and my mother's actions. This was a time of grief, I needed my ex-husband's support, but he was focused on himself.

I didn't understand it, it was crazy to see this, I couldn't fathom it. My mother's behavior was very erratic to me, my ex-husband was upset and demanding attention, and my father was dead. I was mentally and emotionally strained. As time went on I would see their actions become more bizarre. I was only seeing the beginning.

Once my ex lost the church, he dedicated time to finding another church. He worked some odd jobs here and there, but mainly just wanted another church. At this time, I wasn't working, just at home with my daughter and stepson. I was frustrated at not having enough money nor any free time, and my ex was frustrated with not having a church or enough money. He didn't want me to work (that would have helped us financially), but he was against it. Instead, he would constantly ask his mother for money to help with bills and then get angry if she said no.

Eventually, he was able to get another church in the Spartanburg, SC area. This was a very nice and prominent church, and well known. Once he was elected as pastor, he began to work in the church, helping the people, and became a full-time pastor. The church was very giving and understanding because we lived about 3 hours away, so traveling was hard at times. By this time, I had my second child, another girl, and she was only 6 months old. I didn't travel to the church all the time, because of the kids. After about 2 months I noticed that there were some changes happening. For example, my ex was spending more and more time at a young minister's house (this young male minister was 25 years old). My ex used to stay at a hotel instead of driving back when he was tired, but now he was spending the night at the minister's house.

When I confronted him about how much time he was spending away from home, he just responded by saying that he was a full-time pastor and the church needed him there. My gut feeling was that he was lying through his teeth, something wasn't right. I could feel it. Let me say this, when you're married to someone and they're not doing something right, you will feel it. It's an inward feeling and intuition, so to speak, because you have become one. Now, whether we heed to it or not, is up to us.

I kept exploring what I was feeling and believed my ex was having sex with the male minister at the church. I didn't have proof, just my gut feeling. He kept saying he was mentoring him (I finally got proof after we were divorced). Soon, my ex's behavior changed, and I saw the results of his cheating. There was money missing from the bank account, and my ex started wearing thongs, tighter pants, and talked a lot about this young man. He took this guy on a trip to the beach, bought him clothes, and even gave him money. All the while he was neglecting his family. All so he could spend as much time as possible with his lover. It finally got to the point where my ex didn't want me, the kids or any of his family coming to church with him. If I stated that I was coming to church that Sunday, he would get irritated and try to come up with some reason why I shouldn't come.

I know I should have confronted him, but the thing is, when you have been emotionally beaten down by someone and have self-esteem and mental damage from that, you are scared to say anything. Your world is the person you're with because that's how they have trained your mind, basically you're brainwashed.

Of course, my ex was voted out of the church, and of course, he didn't think he should have been voted out. The deacons caught on to what was happening, and the church members too. So, they moved quickly and put him out. The young man stayed in the church, because he was raised in that church.

Now, I know some of you are reading this and asking, didn't I see some signs of him being gay? Did I not notice something different about him?

The answer is yes, I noticed some things about him, but I didn't make an assumption that he was gay. I assumed he had been raised mostly by his mother, because his father worked a lot. Also, I was naive and believed I had a good man, and would be fine with him. I fault myself for not pushing to know more about him. For the most part he told me some things about his past, to include he had a child while in high school. I realize now I chose to be blind and ignore what I did see, in hopes that the relationship would still prosper, because I was in a desperate state. My lesson from that is: **<u>Don't let desperation dictate your decisions.</u>**

After these events, we separated, but the separation was not nice. My ex lied to DSS and said I abandoned my kids. I never abandoned my children!

CHAPTER 5

An explanation

While married to my ex, I was diagnosed with clinical depression. It happened after I gave birth to my first child. My depression was bad, and I would lose interest in doing anything, except sleep. I tried to commit suicide during this time as well because I didn't see a way out of my pain and hurt, and I was mentally lost. He had all the money, I wasn't working, and I was cut off from friends and family. I would spend most of my time with my children and mother-in-law.

Whenever I wanted to go to other places without my ex, he'd tell me I didn't need to go anywhere, and if I did, I needed to take the children with me. Even when I would leave to have my hair done, he'd called my cell phone constantly, asking when I was coming home because he was tired of the kids and had something to do. Sometimes I would only have been gone for 30 minutes, and not even in the stylist chair yet (you ladies understand how it goes at the salon). All of this contributed to my depression, but of course, my ex didn't see that. He told me I was being selfish, and didn't care about the family or him.

He'd belittle me and call me names like "fat bitch, retarded, slow, dumb, the devil, evil, sorry excuse for a wife, no good" and many other things. Then turn around and want me to hug him and have sex with him. If I refused, he accused me of wanting somebody else. Again, these things did not help my depression, they only made it worse. He'd complain when I cooked and then complain when I didn't cook. I couldn't win with him, so eventually, I stopped trying. So, following the advice of my therapist at the time, I would take breaks away from my family, usually at my mother's house or my mother-in-law's house, but never without first making sure it was feasible for my family.

After my ex lost the church, we argued a lot. A month or so later, I took a mental break for a couple of days, and when I returned home, he'd changed the locks and said I couldn't come back to his house. His house! Wow! I thought I could go to my mother's house, but she told me that I wasn't welcome in her home. I found out that she had private conversations with my ex-husband for a long time. She helped to plot to get me out of my own house. I also discovered that she made my ex her power of attorney, while we were still married! My mother has 3 children, in her right mind, so why would she do that? All these things I was finding out at one time. I was definitely in an emotional mess.

I had nowhere to go because my mother didn't want me to live in her house, so I ended up living with my soon to be ex mother-in-law. My mother-in-law welcomed me in and tried to encourage me, but I was hurting because my own mother wasn't supporting me.

To see that your mother didn't support you, and was even working against you, is very hard to process. I couldn't understand it. Family was supposed to be there for you. My brothers were there for me, but my only living parent was not.

I had to go through a divorce, and try to find my own place to stay, and on top of this, I couldn't see my kids because my ex took them and kept them from me. He ended up with primary custody because I didn't have a stable place to live (I was still living with his mother), and the court didn't see that as stable. He said I abandoned the children, and he told the courts that I was mentally incapable of taking care of the children.

My ex used my depression against me. He made me out to be a crazy person, and said that the kids weren't safe around me. He used his status as a preacher and former police officer to influence the decision. Of course, I was angry. I had to have visitations with my kids while this narcissistic idiot kept them full-time!! I also had to pay him child support because it's the law in SC. Whoever the primary parent was, would receive child support from the non-custodial parent. I was beyond pissed. I felt everything was working against me. This man verbally abused me and threatened me for 11 years, and he got to keep my children, get money from me and my mother was supporting him.

When it came time for visitation, he would never show up at the agreed meeting spot. Instead, he'd ghost me, and block my phone number. Then he started telling lies to others in the area, saying that I cheated on him and that's why we were divorced. I did eventually get my own apartment, and thought the children would come. I figured maybe he was mad at his mother and didn't want them to come to her house while I stayed there. He still refused to cooperate. Going to the court yielded no help.

I guess he got tired of not having free time, so he let them visit. I was so glad to see my babies, and they were extremely happy to see me. After a couple of visits, I noticed a difference in their attitude. I soon learned he was talking bad about me to the kids. Telling them that I left them because I didn't want them. I reassured them every time I saw them that I loved them and would never abandon them. Their attitude eventually changed, and we would have an excellent time together.

Oh, but no good time can be had when you co-parent with a narcissist. He would get mad, and go off on angry spells, and hold the children at his house to punish me. For example: he called my phone one day, claiming it was in reference to the children, but he really wanted to talk about himself and what I put him through. I refused to talk about that, so he got mad and blocked my number. When I tried to pick the kids up, he refused to let them come out and would leave the house or threaten me.

Explanation: When you have been brainwashed by a narcissist, you don't become free of that overnight. So, in my mind, I didn't challenge him. I was afraid of not seeing my kids. I felt I had no power, so I had to listen to him. So sometimes, I would sit on the phone and listen to him rant because I didn't want to be without my children. I was still in the mind frame that I had to do what he wanted. Please him, and I get my kids. Make him mad, and I can't see them. As I developed new friendships through work and began therapy, I gained strength and was able to start taking my life back. I understood that I had to fight through the court, even if I felt as if it wasn't working, I had to keep fighting for my children.

CHAPTER 6

The Now

I would love to say that co-parenting with my ex has gotten easier, but it hasn't. Remember, he's a narcissist and still believes that all things are about him. So, whenever he gets angry about anything (this is true), he tries to take it out on me. Instead of getting upset and giving him what he wants, I fight through the court. I refuse to take any of his foolishness. I work with a lawyer to make sure that he complies with the court order. I have strength through my connection with God, and through positive friendships. It's not easy because, at this moment, he still has primary custody, and he tries to overstep his boundaries with it.

CHAPTER 7

Some Lessons Learned

Once you start healing from a narcissistic relationship, you take the power away from them and gain emotional and spiritual strength. The way to handle children that have been turned against you (if you happen to have children with a narcissist), is to remain consistent. Never stop telling them you love them, show up, call, use the legal system and show them that you will never give up on them.

The other lesson is to not engage with a narcissist, meaning keep the conversation short and to the topic, don't allow him or her to steer you away from the point of the conversation.

The biggest lesson from being married to this man, is that I was not the name he called me, I was and I am so much more. I just allowed myself to believe his lies for a long time. When I finally got free, I promised myself I would stay free, not only physically but inwardly as well. True freedom, dear reader, comes from accepting the bad with the good, knowing you're not perfect (or even expecting yourself to be perfect), and being comfortable with it. This is something no one in the world can take from you.

Thank you for reading my story, well, part of my story. There is more, and that I will publish later. Much love to you!!

Acknowledgments

"I want to express my gratitude to God for giving me the strength to write this. It wasn't easy, and to be honest I had my doubts, but I'm glad He made it possible."

TO MY CHILDREN

I know you have suffered as well, and have endured emotional scarring from these events, but I want you to know that no matter what happens in life you can overcome, and you do not have to stay in a toxic relationship, your mother is proof of that.

TO MY BROTHERS

Jamie Leach and Chris Leach. You have been supportive and encouraging to me all my life, and I thank you. I love you both.

I am also grateful for you. You are taking the time to read about my life, and time isn't something we have a lot of. So thank you for sharing some of that time with me by reading this book.

www.ingramcontent.com/pod-product-compliance
Lightning Source LLC
Chambersburg PA
CBHW071313130726
47997CB00007B/2535